LANGAN
MAE

ALSO BY AARON DONLEY

GOOD CHEMISTRY

THE STARLIGHT INN

VISIT AARONDONLEY.COM FOR MORE

WHAT WE ONCE CALLED OUT IN PASSING CLOUDS

by Aaron Donley

LANGAN MAE

LANGAN
MAE

Langan Mae
PO Box 883
Creswell, Oregon 97426

All works by Aaron Donley
Cover and Illustrations by Aaron Donley
Back cover photo by Jenni Donley

Fonts used in this book:
Rockwell (cover)
Theano Didot
Garamond
(Nymphette)

For more information/to sign up for the newsletter visit:
aarondonley.com
To contact for writing/speaking engagements:
langanmae@gmail.com

10 9 8 7 6 5 4 3 2 1

ISBN 978-0-9978997-3-3 (print)
ISBN 978-0-9978997-2-6 (ebook)

Also, for Jenni

THE MASTER

Probably when Michelangelo was intensely working on
sculpting David's genitals someone would walk in the
room and he'd jump and pretend to be working on the
inner thighs. What? What is it? What do you want?
Don't you people ever think to knock??
I'm workin' here!

A MAN, NO PLAN

The word "palindrome" spelled backwards is "emordlinap." Which, when looked up in the dictionary reads: "See, this is why girls don't like you."

LOYALTY

I think fat friends are more loyal than skinny friends. Because when you're surrounded by fat friends, there's a higher probability one of them will take a bullet for you.

REGRETS, HE'S HAD A FEW

I f you were a Bigfoot at a barbeque and walked through the screen door, you'd probably feel the need to cover your embarrassment by running around growling and chasing people with the wire mesh. It really sucks too, because that's not what you were trying to be.

WE LOVE YOU CLEVELAND

I think the big mistake most acid rockers make is they claim to have heard my town likes to rock. No, you see, we used to like to rock, but that was a long time ago. We were young...it was the war...we'd rather not talk about it.

TAKE FLIGHT

❦

As I jumped from the airplane, I thought I'd never see my family again. But somehow they found me, hiding in the museum gift shop.

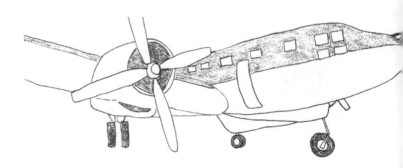

SWEET RELIEF

O ur first day on the new planet after we ruin
this one, go ahead and litter something
just to break the ice. The tension must be
unbearable.

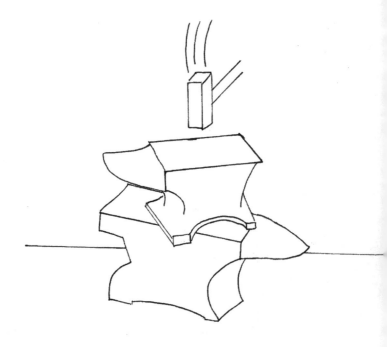

TAKE IT EASY

When making your first anvil the reality is you'll have to swallow your pride and borrow another anvil to do the job. Now you're thinking, "Maybe I'll just take my embarrassment out on the new anvil, *no one will notice.*" Hold it right there. You, and you alone, are to blame for improper anvil planning.

OH YEAH, I KNOW HOW I LIKE IT

I bet

in the asexual

plant community,

novelty pens

turn upside down

to slowly reveal

naked pictures

of themselves.

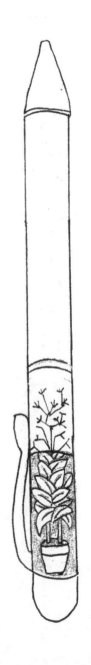

WONDERFULLY MADE

They say a newborn's brain has over one hundred
times the processing speed of the most powerful
computer on earth. Wow. Isn't it amazing we're on
the verge of finally making baby brains obsolete?
The world's first baby brain computer;
it's gonna blow your baby's mind.

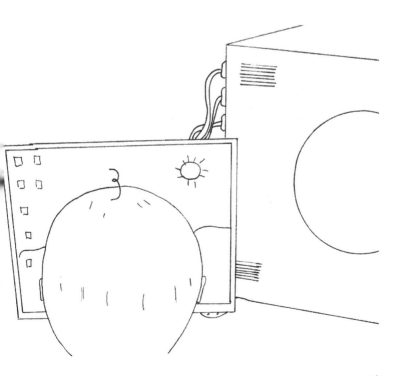

THE MESSAGE

I like to attach messages to balloons

and have them drift over to where

funerals are taking place.

"We come back as balloons,

warn everyone."

They say.

BANJO

I think a lot of people who torture banjo players are just tortured banjo players themselves. It's their way of getting close to banjo.

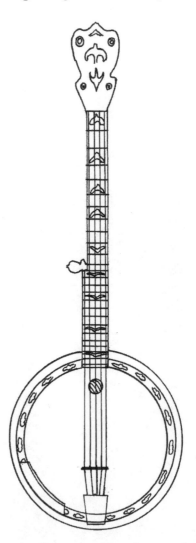

ALL THEY HAD

I come from a long line of bean counters. Not a one of them had any financial sense though. You can't sit up in the attic all day counting beans and expect the checkbook to balance itself. I don't even think they could count the beans. It's like they'd just sort of sit up there and push them from side to side. It was all they had.

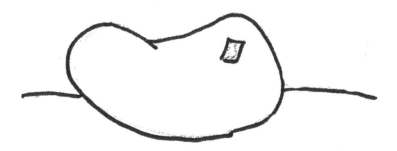

LITTLE STORY ABOUT JOHN AND ANNA

Anna's wealthy father strictly forbade her from being with John, a misunderstood greaser from across the tracks. They had only exchanged glimpses and quick remarks before tonight, but everything was about to change. John shut off the engine of his 76' Chevy as he coasted down her driveway. Anna climbed out of her bedroom window. They were free. Five miles out of town they pulled over and embraced. As passions ran hot their eyes met and they both knew what the other wanted, -A frank discussion about how they were only in this for the novelty aspect. Both of them cited an onset of diarrhea*, and they drove back to town.

*Only a part lie as Anna felt a poop coming on.

ADVICE ON JIMMY CARTER

If you happen across the dead body of former President Jimmy Carter and discover what those in the mortuary business term a "death boner," take a picture with the boner, being careful to avoid pretension, for he is a Man of Plains.

RINGS A BELL

First phone call in history:
BELL: "Mr. Watson, come here, I want to see you."
WATSON: "What, we have to call ahead now before stopping by? Whatever happened to the pop-in? Are you telling me the pop-in is dead?"

Second phone call in history:
BELL: "Watson stop fooling around!"
WATSON (sarcastically): "Who is this?"

Third phone call in history:
BELL: "Watson!"
WATSON: (In Arabic accent.): "Ali Baba's house of noodle. Ali speaking."

IMPRESSIVE

A great thing to have done when they were starting to tear down the Berlin Wall would have been to secretly replace their wrecking ball with an identical ball made of silly putty. Then when the ball smushed against the wall, you could stand there proudly and yell, "Now that's what I call a wall!"

A SPECIAL DAY

My parents always tried to make birthdays special. Like the time they bought me a cake with some other kid's name on it. "That's not my name!" I cried. "Yes it is," they said. It was then dad motioned down to the sticker on the lid; "*half-off special.*" Mom held firm.

SETTING PARAMETERS

If humans learn to fly, I would be cool with letting the blind soar at high altitudes, free of wires and buildings

PERFORMANCE ANXIETY

The bonsai plant sat perched on the store window
ledge, ready to leap into the freedom of the outside.
But what battle cry to yell during the triumphant
escape? The question puzzled it into a frozen state
of panic as the store owner shut the window and
relocated the plant into the weed and feed aisle.

CRIMES AGAINST HUMANITY

I think people who commit crimes against humanity should have to commit an equal amount of crimes for humanity so the humanity crime total remains balanced.

PLAY IT COOL

When tipping your hat to a cross-eyed cowboy, don't over exaggerate the tip. He's not blind you know.

WORK

I recently had an old guy tell me,

"Life ain't a bowl of cherries, son.
You gotta work!"

Well, I told him
that picking
a whole bowl of cherries by myself
sounded like
hard work to me.

Then I took a nap.

Old people make me tired.
What with their incessant talk
of bowls
and cherries,
and work.

THE COLLECTOR

They say

we only use

10 percent

of our brains,

but I say

the goal

is to collect,

not use

the brains.

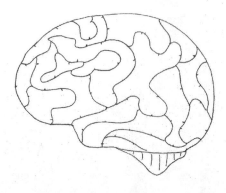

PLANS

I don't think we should be teaching the elderly how to use technology as much how to submit to technology during the replacement process.

WORDS GOING
THROUGH MIND:

1. INFERNAL

2. CONTRAPTION

ACCESSORIES

I think the thing to remember when accessorizing a chastity belt is, work to make it warm and inviting.

SAFETY NET

I think cigarette companies should seriously think about making one of every ten or so packs really addictive. Just to provide a safety net for themselves in these uncertain times.

ASTOUNDING

Isn't it amazing that what we once called out in passing clouds as bunnies and turtles could have been, without fail, more accurately identified as 'cancerous tumors'? Our error rates must have been astounding.

RESPECT

If I were a streaker,

    my accessory of choice,

        would be one clown shoe.

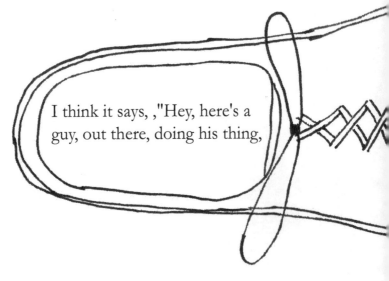

I think it says, ,"Hey, here's a guy, out there, doing his thing,

    but keeping it fun at the same time

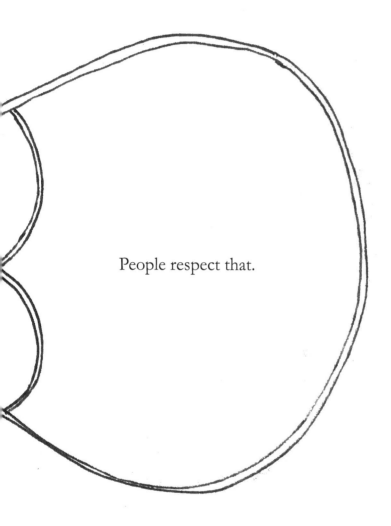

People respect that.

COMMON

O ne thing you always have to like about the common cold is its persistence. Year after year it remains number one on the infectious disease list, training tirelessly in the offseason with only one goal permanently fixed on its laser-focused mind: being number one. Common? I don't think so. Not in this day and age.

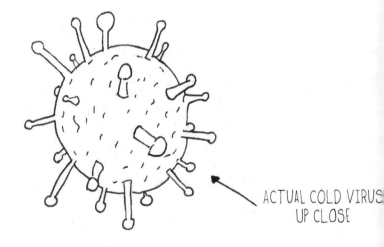

ACTUAL COLD VIRUS
UP CLOSE

TERROR

I f I were going to make a scary horror flick I would probably start off by showing a little girl baking cookies. Seem harmless? Well, not when you discover that with the rising cost of education her father's factory worker salary will likely only support her through a state college.

COMEDY GOLD

If you are a disgruntled court jester

feeling an outcast for having

what was considered to be

'off-color' material,

just sort of casually

bide your time

until a big battle.

Then secretly replace

the King's sword

so when he pulls it out

and yells,

"For the Queen!!,"

there'd be

a jumbo tampon in its place.

(Now that's what I call comedy.)

BELLY ITCHER

ack Taylor pitched the ball under hand to the children in the Dads vs. Kids Little League game. But who was he kidding? Jack had always thrown like a girl and everybody knew it. He was getting creamed out there folks. A more pitiful display the town could not recall.

A POEM: COMMON COURTESY

If your blind date
speaks through a hole in her throat,
be courteous
and 'defer to the hole'
when requesting a lozenge.

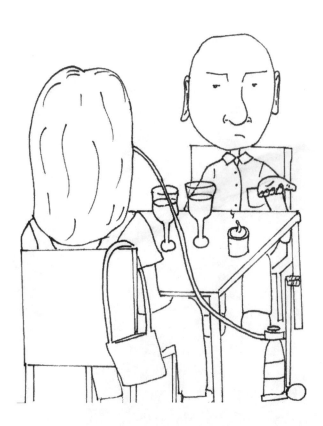

HINDSIGHT

It's too bad Velma's guardian angel has a top highway speed of 27 mph. That little piece of information would have been helpful to know before applying the bumper sticker.

IT'S THEIR DAY

I would like to cater a cannibal wedding banquet and just sort of slip a cow tongue in with the others. Deception is wrong, but it's also their day ya' know?

THE TRUTH IS OUT THERE

The question is not "Who made the crop circles?" As we all know, they're made by those crazy UFO enthusiasts in the dark of night using flat boards they walk on with strings on each end. The real question is, "When and how did the aliens transmit the blueprints and technology involved in creating these 'board-with-string' devices?"

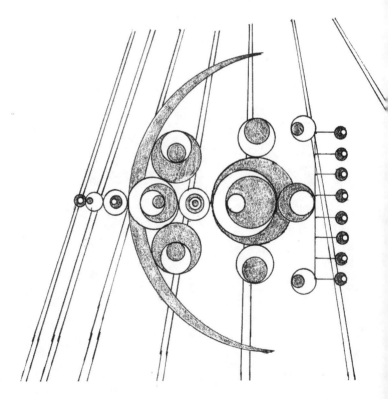

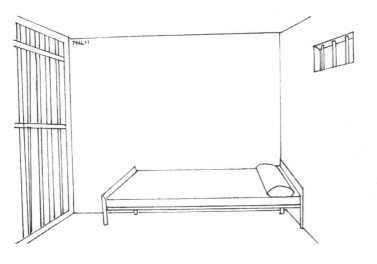

OPTIMISM

I t's interesting how death row inmates will initially start their daily tally marks high up on their cell walls. Simple death row inmate, it's that kind of wide-eyed optimism that got you there in the first place.

'NAM

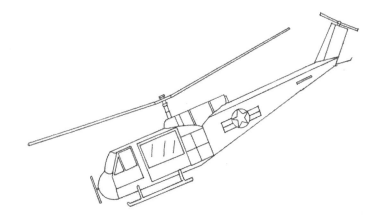

What people

fail to realize,

is that when I speak

of my service in 'Nam,'

I'm referring to my time spent

as a waiter

at a Denny's,

in Nam, Iowa.

It's a little town

50 miles west

of Des Moines.

Yeah, me and my buddy Charlie had some pret-ty

tough customers at times.

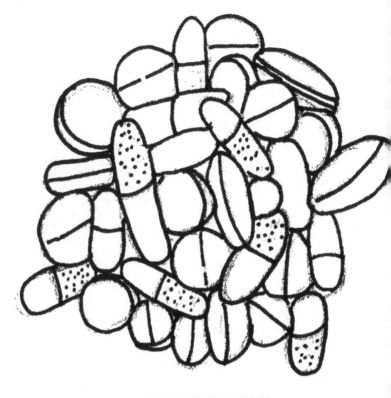

ON BEING FAT

I wonder how many diet pills would it take for someone to get fat off of them?

FOR THIS VERY REASON

I f you were drilling a hole to the center of the earth, it would be really discouraging to discover that your drill bit was exactly one inch too short. And that they make them that length for this very reason.

THE DINGER

L et's say you were a mute addicted to dinging your water glass in crowded restaurants. So ding for a few minutes, they will give you that, you're a mute. But then pause with the fork next to the glass and keep them waiting in silence until the point they can no longer stand it. Then do a soft ding.

RESPECT

P robably the biggest complaint from most cavemen book editors had to do with the relentless parade of autobiographies opening with the first time the author went on a hunt with his father and witnessed a dinosaur in full force urination. Powerful, yes. But you see, there's a building up process here you're ignoring. It's about respecting the reader.

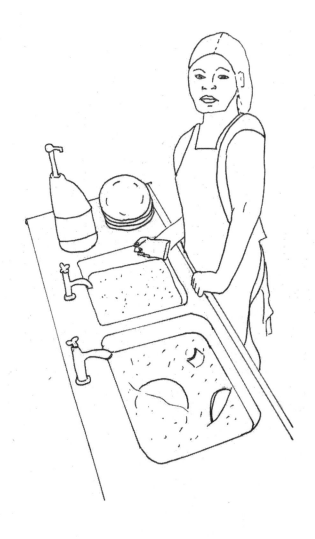

THE COOL MOVE

I f you have to wash dishes because you can't
pay a restaurant bill, I think a cool move would
be to gently reach down under the water and
passionately squeeze your date's hand.
Then hand her a dish.

THE RUNAWAY

The runaway sat watching the train go by. Is this what his life had become? A series of days spent sleeping, nights spent in a free-for-all drunken stupor? Why didn't he work during the day like everyone else? Then, in 40 years he could retire and get to sleep all day and spend his nights in a free for all drunken stupor. Feeling better about his life choices he went back to sleep. Soon however, nightfall came and he was awoken by a sniffing dog. Go away dog, he thought. But then he had an idea. He killed the dog and ate it by firelight. Dog by firelight; a hobo delicacy.

ON GARDENING

T he only thing that beats the joy of gardening is the boredom of gardening, which is why I don't do it.

THE DOLPHIN AND THE WHALE

I think a good cartoon would be about a dolphin and a whale. Then at the end they stare into the camera and make you feel bad about the racial overtones.

I BET YOU DIDN'T KNOW THAT

Here's something you didn't know. If you ever get stranded, remember that you can drink your own urine. In fact, you know what? Better go ahead and pack some bottled urine before the trip just in case. Oh, people may say, "Why not just pack extra water?" Why? You'll say. Because you can drink your own urine. I bet you didn't know that.

THE GIVER

Tried to feed a duck a rock, but he didn't go for it. So I kicked it over his way again. Still nothing. "It's bread, duck," I quacked. "Nourishment for the soul." Finally he ate it. Man, I give and give.

ADDING VALUE THROUGH CONTEXT

W hen placing a dunce cap on a toddler, explaining the rich historical context of the cap in a way they can understand can add so very much.

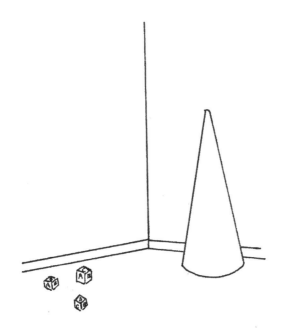

THE BRIGHT IDEA

W hen Thomas Edison first got the idea for the light bulb, I wonder if a candle went on over his head.

A FRIENDLY REMINDER

I think the pregnant silence when an Olympic figure skater is waiting to see her results might be a good time to remind everyone of the dangers of elephantitis. Nothing special, maybe just a few graphic photos and some testimonials to drive the point home. Which is that it could happen to you anywhere, at any time, for no reason. And now for the results...

MEMORIES

I bet if you could remember being born, the thing that would stick out most would be how little scrubs have changed.

THE TALE OF THE MAD HORSEMAN

People think the mad horseman is only thirsty for blood. But what if the horse has Cushing's disease? It is incurable. However with medicine and a monitored diet the horse can still live a normal life.

S'ARRGHY MAN

I f you wear an eye patch but can prove you already
owned a parrot before the loss of the eye... Man,
I still think you're going to have to get rid of the
parrot.

A FISH PARABLE

One time I was on my way to give this guy his daily fish so he could eat. And I thought, "Wait a minute, am I getting suckered? Maybe I should just teach him how to fish. Then he could eat for a lifetime." Well, I had to laugh at myself, because I remembered that he's the one who taught me how to fish, in exchange for providing him one fish a day for a lifetime. Sucker. So I continued on my delivery, but had to stop and laugh again. Not because of anything special, only that I noticed the fish I was carrying seemed to have the queerest little smile on his face you ever saw. I tried to mimic it, but he stopped.

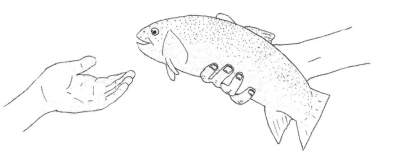

DAMAGE CONTROL

When invading a tribal culture for the first time,
remember not to poop out the side of the helicopter
on the initial fly by. Because, can you even imagine the
psychological damage?

THE FINAL HUDDLE

I'll never forget the last team huddle of the big game when our coach, nearly in tears, said, "Boys, it's not whether you win or lose. It's how you play the game that counts." Knowing the hearts and mind of all the fellas, I spoke first. "What about the game of Russian roulette?" I had stumped him. Stumped him good.

YOUR LUCKY DAY

If you find a four leaf clover and someone hits you over the head and steals it, you're still pretty lucky I didn't use a tire iron.

LIFE, LIBERTY, PURSUIT OF HAPPINESS?

❦

I bet when they finally invent a baby muzzle they'll probably have to put an emergency button on it for the baby to activate. So much for living in a 'free country.'

ASPIRATIONS

Y ou see this coin? The old main said, raising the Fruit Loop. Then, peering through its hole continued, "I found this off the coast of Chili, buried ten feet down at the bottom of the ocean. It's worth *a billion dollars.*" Wow, thought the male nurse changing his diaper. I want to be like this guy someday. More so for him having a large penis than the coin, though.)

SOME PEOPLE

If there was one thing Grandpa hated
most about the blacks and the Jews,
it was how they'd look down on him
when he'd urinate in public.

YOU CAN'T CHANGE WHO YOU ARE

As I was counseling the homeless gentleman, I began to realize he was a "bottle is half empty" kind of guy. He insisted that he wasn't, but I knew better. I had already taken his bottle and drunken half by then.

THE OLD HANGMAN

The old hangman loved his gallows. He loved walking the stairs in the early sunlight and resting his calloused hand on the lever. He called the lever "Eric," which made people think he was gay. But he was not gay, he just named the lever after his penis. "Why name your penis Eric if you are not gay?" the townspeople would say. "Because I once knew a man named Eric who had a great penis'" he would say. "But, how would you even know that?" they would say. "Don't worry about it, I just know," he would say. "Listen, we don't even care if you're gay, in fact we would applaud you for coming out. Just tell us!" "Not gay," he would mumble, continuing his knitting work on a new hood. "Ok, let's just start over," the townspeople would take a collective deep breath, "So being gay is great isn't it, huh?" But the old man was no longer listening. From his vantage point atop the gallows he could survey the town as a whole, both with its good penises and bad. A rooster could be heard in the distance sparking his mind to wander to simpler times when, as a child he used to wring their necks. He wished he had never known of Eric or his penis. Furthermore he wished he had never named the lever Eric. He really wasn't gay, but now it seemed like he was being down on gays if he made a big deal about it either way.

Each evening the moonlight would shine down on the old gallows just outside his bedroom window, "Night gallows," he'd whisper before rolling over. Beside him sat a tiny gallows he had whittled. "Eric" was a matchstick, which looked like a penis.

EXCERPTS: A FAREWELL TO ARMS BY ERNEST HEMINGWAY

Page 132- *Bill and his father worked the fishing vessel for many years together. One day Bill's arm was ripped off in a net. As it was sinking to the depths his father came to him and said, "I'm sorry son. I know how you liked that arm." "One of my favs," Bill replied.*

Page 198- *John had worked around heavy machinery at the mill all his life. On this day it was his job to un-snag chunks of wood from the giant 8 ft diameter blade so they wouldn't have to shut down the line. His arm got ripped off in the glass door turnstile at the bank later when he went to cash his check.*

Page 301 -*The giant dragon with fifteen arms terrorized the city, eating its inhabitants and burning their buildings with his fire-breathing mouth. In that town, a man owned an oak furniture store. And in that furniture store he only sold chairs with high arm rests. He went out of business. They were very impractical.*

I MEAN SERIOUSLY

Probably the biggest reasons why people stopped traveling in blimps were the high-grade but outdated dinnerware present, and the Hindenburg explosion. High grade, yes. But outdated? Did they think people wouldn't notice?

IT WAS TIME HE KNEW

I'll never forget the day I had to put my horse down. He was never going to amount to anything and I felt like he should know it.

THE HITCHHIKER

Katy nervously studied the dark stranger she had hitched a ride with on the lonely road outside of town. It was then that she noticed the severed heads in the backseat. Later that night she would wipe away his tears, for no one had ever cared about his heads before.

MOTIVATION

I find it helpful to occasionally go downtown and present one of the bums down there with a motivational poster of a bunch of white guys rowing a boat, with the word GOALS printed on the bottom. "You see those guys rowing?" I'll say. "Not bad, eh?" Sometimes I'll even lie and say one of the rowers is me. You'll see me standing there with my hands in my pockets, staring out at the horizon, "Yeah you could say I've lived a *pret-ty* successful life."

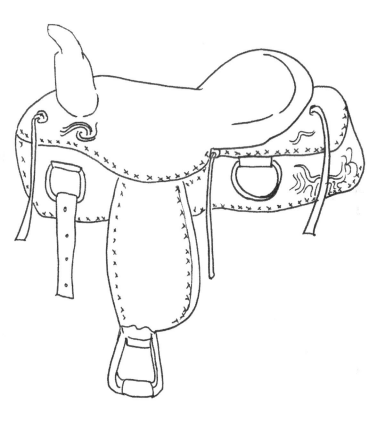

PULLING BACK THE REINS

I don't think people who say horses are the 'love
of their lives' should be allowed to ride bare back.
Because how far are we going to let this thing go?

OUT OF THE BOX

I think a good present for a child is a jack in the box where no matter how hard they try the jack won't pop out. Then on your death bed you can hold up the jack and say something really important.

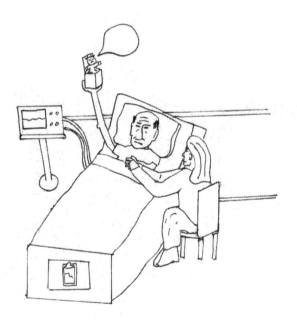

OUR FUTURE?

It's 3 a.m. and you're up again, worrying about investing too much money in your kids' education. Are they really our future? 'Something has to be done,' you whisper. Then, you crack a scheme to secretly begin shaving a little off the top each year into a separate account labeled 'adults only.' C'mon, they're kids… They'll never figure it out. Especially with the education they'll be getting.

RAINDROPS

As the rain

beat against my window

I thought,

if I could stop

those people outside

from yelling,

"Dad, let us in!"

I would.

GNASHING OF TEETH

Upon my death I'd like to pay my subjects a salary for weeping in my honor. But don't pay the poor too much because they only got good at weeping because of my reign.

CHALLENGING YOUR KIDS

Want to get your kids thinking about math? Next time one asks you if they're, 'ever going to use this in real life,' say, "Well, I doubt *you'll* ever have to use it." That'll get them thinking.

WHO BUTTERS YOUR BREAD?

They say don't bite the hand that feeds you.

Which is precisely why I stopped

biting my nails.

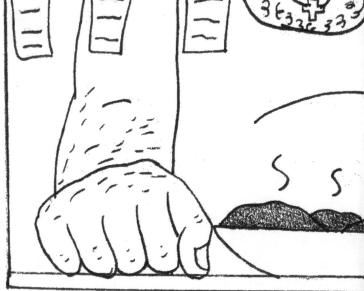

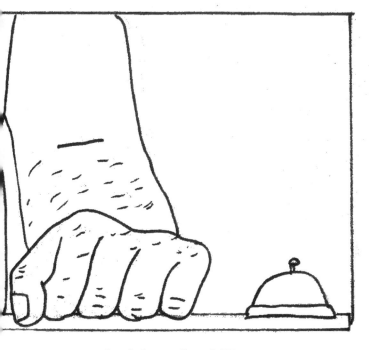

And the nails of Horace,

the night cook

at the Koffee Kup Diner.

IN THE LAND OF GIANTS

If you were a midget giant in the land of giants, hearing you explain how you're, 'still pretty tall,' would get old real fast.

AH.. NOSTALGIA

Remember the good old days? When during the heat of summer we'd skinny dip down at Roger's Creek and hitch a ride home in the back of some old farmer's truck? Then the whole gang would spend the rest of the day playin' ball and drinking pop in the shade of Rolley Henderson's big oak tree? And later, we'd all sneak out behind the drive-in and play pranks on the older kids carousing in the back seats of their parent's cars? Remember those times? Yeah, me neither.

IF YOU BELIEVE...

The phrase people always use
when something breaks down is,
"How can they put a man on the moon,
and they still can't make a good
(hair dryer, waffle iron, etc.)?!"

I think maybe it's time,
we just accepted,
that putting a man on the moon,
wasn't that hard.

OUT OF THE BIG TOP

Jennie stared out the window of the bus, grasping her one-way ticket to a new life full of possibilities.

Twisting her mustache as they passed the circus tents,
they now seemed so small...

THE LIE

I felt weird

telling the people

at the party

that I peed my pants

from laughing so hard.

Because I knew

deep down

it was

just a little dribble.

TRUTH BE TOLD

The most difficult thing about joining a liars anonymous group has got to be the pressure of coming up with a believable testimony. Because let's be honest, you're dealing with professionals here. Any variance towards the extraordinary or overly mundane would immediately give you away as a rank amateur. It would probably be a wise move to steer clear of any fish stories or tales of sexual prowess as well. It can be a tough room, there's no doubt. But the reward of hearing genuine applause and respect from a bunch of liars for a job well done makes it all worthwhile.

WITH THE BEARS

J ack abandoned all to go live in the wilderness with the bears. After several months of staying at a distance, one day he strangely felt their welcoming him in. For example, a fish was placed at his tent door one morning. Then, some wild honey was placed near his campfire. Eventually his hopes where confirmed as they invited him into their pack. Not long after he would marry one of them in a simple ceremony and soon had a family of bear-children. One day, however, he awoke to find his wife and the cub-kids had left him for a real bear. Broken hearted, he returned to society and became a bum. It was the same life basically, just without the bears. You see, he didn't want anything to do with bears after that.

THE LOCH NESS MONSTER

I don't believe in the Loch Ness Monster.

In fact, I have virtually no confidence at all in his ability to accomplish even the simplest of tasks.

Oh, he knows he's a failure. You can see it in his eyes.

You'll catch him sitting there, looking up at the night sky, questioning his very existence.

LOLLIPOP MIKE

My childhood friend, "Lollipop Mike" was actually
allergic to lollipops. In fact that's how he got his
name, because he died a horrible death of "lollipop
poisoning." I tried to coin the phrase, "The Lou
Gehrig of Lollipop Poisoning," at his funeral but
those punks have no of sense of the moment.
They wouldn't even call him "Lollipop Mike."
My God is it tough to coin a phrase these days.

A MAN OF FEW WORDS

I've found women are often attracted to a man of few words, until they're told the actual number of words you know, no matter how low that number may be.

AN UNDERSTANDING

If a man walks tall,

go ahead and let him.

And if he walks tall with a really tall hat on,

still let him,

but with an understanding between you

about the hat.

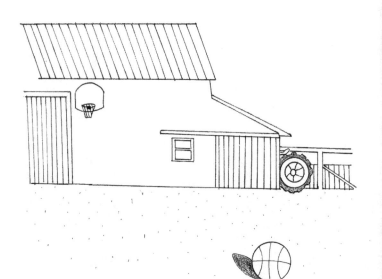

THIS KID'S GONNA MAKE IT

Nothing could stop young Matt Dressikie from achieving his dreams of being a pro basketball player. Not the amputation of his arms and legs, or the fact he came from a nowhere town in rural Indiana. His father, a former semi-pro player embittered by his missed chances, would often tell Matthew, "Son, you can give your life and blood to this game, and all it will give you in return is heartache. Pure heartache." Yet this did not deter him. Even the discouragement of his coach didn't take his eyes off the goal. "Get you head out of the clouds, boy!" his coach would say. "Ain't nobody from this town ever gonna make it to the big-time." Matt's peers would often make fun and put down his dreams, "Look at him," they'd point. "He has big dreams. He thinks he's too good for us." Still, Matt held on to them. For one day he was going to prove them all wrong. Yes folks, this quadruple amputee was gonna make it.

TRUE HORROR

Indeed, the most terrifying thing about medieval times that even the goriest of movies are afraid to show, is the unforgiving, relentless body odor of everyone present.

A SIMPLE TEST

I would like to get a bunch of nice guys in a race and see who finishes last. (Probably the nicest one.)

AS A MATTER OF COURTESY

For all-midget sex scenes, kindly tape a penny next to their genitals to aid the viewer with a relative sense of scope and size.

AGAINST ALL ODDS

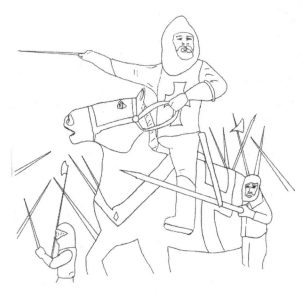

The men marched up the hill, full well knowing what lay on the other side: the enemy army. Ten thousand strong against their two hundred. Knowing the odds against them, the commander declared, "If anyone is scared, he should speak up now." Everyone spoke at once and created such a noise the enemy camp awoke from their slumber and proceeded to massacre them all in quick time. It was a numbers game, really.

In fact the massacre was so fast that after the enemy army returned to bed, they awoke the next morning and thought it might have all been a dream. "Nope!" one of them shouted, pointing to the still smoldering mound of carcasses on the hillside.

A RARE AND MUCH RESPECTED TRICK

Let's say you're breast feeding
and at the same time
a mosquito bites your baby.

I bet mosquitoes call that
the, "double human suck-suck."

117

THE GREAT SPIRIT HAS SPOKEN

Will one day civilized mankind so plunder the natural resources of our land that they will cease to exist, therefore allowing for Native American tribes to once again be risen by the Great Spirit to cultivate and return harmony to our earth as it was in days past? The answer is no.

DON'T STRAIN YOURSELF

If you have a neck brace and see a cute girl also wearing one, acknowledge, but don't nod up and down too much because it makes you seem desperate.

REAL ABUSE

"No animals
were harmed
during the making
of this film."

Yes, perhaps.
But might not
the real abuse lie
in our hindering
of their ability
to grow
from said adversities?

NOT BLOODY LIKELY

Brady asked his Scottish commander
who was sending him into battle,
"Are the chances of not getting bloody, likely?"

> "Is not getting bloody
> likely?" the commander repeated,
> "Not bloody likely!
> Now get in there and fight!"

Well Brady took one
look at the battle and
yelled, "Not bloody likely!!"
and ran away.

> But then, as he was running,
> his longtime friend,
> John "Bloody" Likely
> was shot down
> in front of him.

"Not Bloody Likely!!" Brady yelled,

ROYALTY

Whilst observing head council members amid their varied comings and goings about the nudist colony, do take note of their distinguished gait.

FINANCIAL PLANNING

H al had always followed his father's advice to set aside a penny each day for retirement. So you can imagine his surprise when he went to cash it all in and had exactly $127 to retire on. That was dumb, he thought.

A POEM: FOR ADVANCED MANEUVERING

⚬ഖ⚬ഖ⚬

Always pick the girl

in gym class

square dancing

who most resembles

a square.

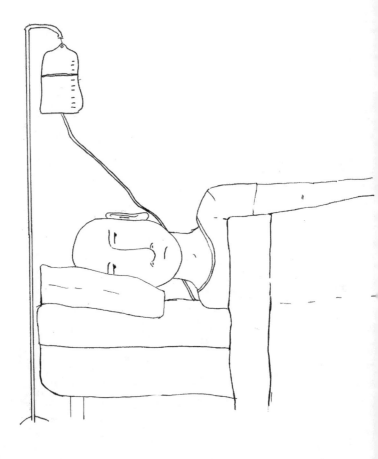

IT'S BEST

If you awake from a coma to find the nurse wiping you, it's best to 'fake the coma' for a few more minutes until he's finished.

THE GREATEST TRICK OF ALL

The old magician studied his wand. *So you are what has kept me from having sex with women*, he thought

THE ONE EYED DOG

I'll never forget the one-eyed dog behind the neighbor's fence I had to pass on my way to school each day. I'd heard of how one eyed dogs can go mad from the absence of full sight. How it affects their brain over time and makes them paranoid and predatory, especially if you make eye contact. I knew not to take any chances, so I started throwing my lunch over the fence as I ran by just to make peace. *"I ain't got no business with you one-eyed mad dog!"* I'd scream. One day the dog died, and somehow a part of me felt strangely without closure. So I visited his grave site and placed a final sandwich on his tombstone. Maybe he had two eyes.

A MESSAGE

If you overflow a public toilet, I think it's ok to leave a note saying 'God did it.' Because who's to know what that might mean to someone?

YOU AIN'T SO BAD

I think we should get back to burying our fat people in piano boxes. Hey genius classical pianists, check out what we're doing with your boxes. So... also I don't like you.

YOU'RE BETTER THAN THAT

When writing clown erotica, don't, "honk noses," too much. It's a bit heavy handed.

SOCIETY

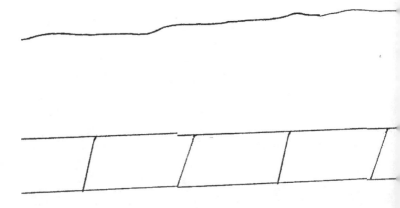

I'd like to go to a park and set a beautiful baby doll next to a real baby with an ugly face. You should be ashamed of yourself, society.

EXCERPTS: PILGRIM AT TINKER CREEK
BY ANNIE DILLARD

Page 42

I first spotted him down there the other day. That pilgrim. With his pilgrim hat and pilgrim shoes and pilgrim smile. He was rummaging around for something. Maybe turnips or something stupid like a pilgrim would eat. While he was washing his feet I took one of his shoes. You should have seen that stupid pilgrim grin fade when he saw one of them was missing. He could tell it'd been stolen too because there was a big imprint in the mud next to the other shoe. Later, as he was sitting downcast by the river wearing the lone shoe, a rock whizzed by his head, knocking his hat clear into the drink.

WANTING TO BELIEVE

The one thing all first-time airline pilots have in common, regardless of training, is they spend a good 45 minutes wanting to believe the on-board toilets empty directly to the outside, disintegrating their contents into thin air.

RUDE AWAKENING

What would be really disappointing would be to have finally had that breakthrough conversation with your cell mate where you both open up with complete honesty and acceptance. Then, just as you're really making progress, the other guy asks you to "hold that thought for just a second." He gets up, goes over to the stainless toilet you both share, and carefully places tissue paper around the lid before using. Wake up call: you're in prison, buddy.

THE PROPRIETOR

If I were the proprietor of an opium den, I think I would just sort of casually set out free poppy seed muffins in the kids' play area. And if any of the parents came to me and asked, 'Just what the heck I thought I was doing.' I would say, 'Oh yeah, like you're a good parent or something.'

FIEND

THE VICTIMS

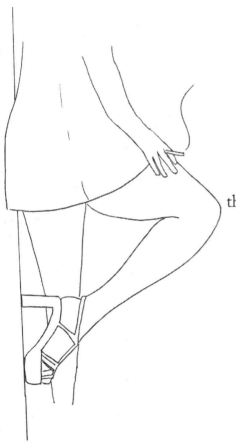

I find it sad
these days
that many prostitutes
will just use men,
for their money.

ONE GOOD DEED DESERVES

As I helped the old lady across the street I was re-
minded of my Great-Aunt Edna, who pushed me into
moving traffic one time when I was a kid.

LEARN FROM THIS

It took me weeks to convince my buddy Randy to dress up as a clown for my kid's birthday party. Then, when he showed up there was no party. Well I had to laugh, having out clowned a clown. It's called a life lesson, Bobo. I mean, Randy.

QUIET BEAUTY; A POEM

Her quiet beauty

was like

a sewage plant,

which has just installed

the ultra-quiet

3000 GXN model

industrial septic pump unit.

The very pump

called, 'a thing of beauty,'

by Sewage Monthly Magazine.

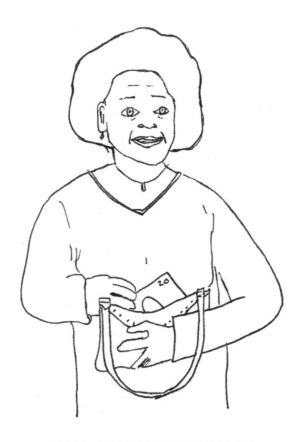

HAPPY MOTHER'S DAY

I could never repay my mom for all the wonderful
things she's done. Like loan me money.

LISTEN

Some people say I only contracted the tapeworm so I could take full advantage of the all-you-can-eat buffet at Sizzler. Well, those people are wise. You should listen to them.

KING OF THE WOMB

If

you were a newborn

who

had absorbed your twin's fetus in the womb,

don't

be too flippant on your first

burp.

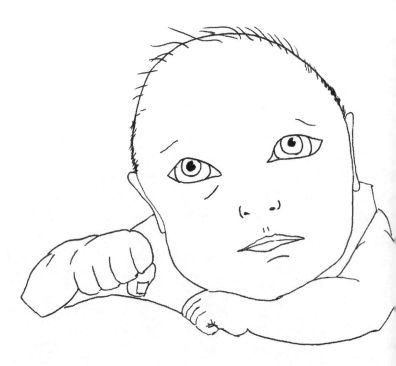

STANDARDS

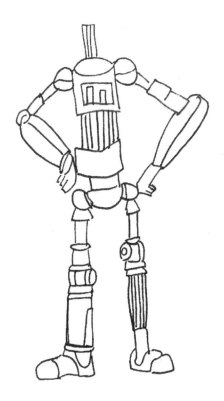

When I die I want my head to be frozen, then re-thawed and placed on the body of a robot. And if the robot has had many other heads before tell it I am not, "that kind of head." This head is a one-robot head.

THE TESTER

You know how down at the rubber band factory there's that guy who tests all the rubber bands to make sure they're not too tight or too loose? Anyway, I bet he gets really cocky with it, too. Man, I'd probably hate that guy.

UM, YEAH IT'S MINE

It would be really unfortunate if you vomited in a spaceship. Because there it would be, floating around the whole time, making people feel incomfortable.

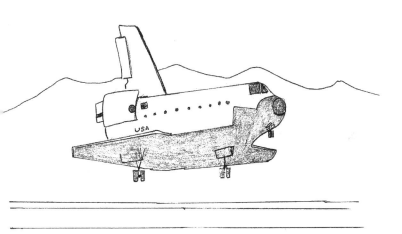

GO TO SLEEP

Imagine the joy of tucking in your first robot child. "But I do not sleep," it would say. I know, robot child, I know. Just pretend to sleep for me though, ok? "I do not understand, 'pretend?'" Shhhh, you would say, putting your hand over its voice register and pulling up the covers. Then, before shutting the door all the way, you look back at those beady eyes staring at you through the darkness and whisper, "You're replaceable."

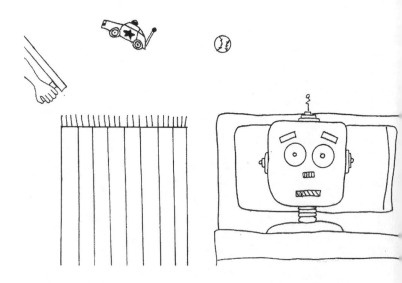

GAZING THROUGH THE GRATE

Like a stream

of arched golden liquid,

the morning sunshine

"urinated"

over the sewer dweller's face.

JOY

The joy of shoplifting

is something money

just can't buy.

KARMA

As I sped up to hit the skinny cow on the road I
wondered if it was his fault or mine.

GET LOST IN IT

For slash and burn farming, nothing will do but heavy metal. Yes, just put on the heavy metal and you're good to go. You'll be slashing. You'll be burning. Sometimes for hours you know? Listen, you're there anyway, get lost in it.

TIME TO GROW UP

I think flesh-colored diapers are a good way to start transitioning newborns out of a "nudity is ok" mindset.

ADVICE ON SHOOTING MONKEYS

~

If you're going to shoot a monkey, make sure you do it in the head, execution-style. If, say, you shoot them in the stomach or groin, they'll just mope around and bleed a lot. That monkey is no good for anyone.

Do it quick. With a .30 caliber or better. Never use a shotgun. Trust me. You also might want to think about tranquilizers. Not to make him totally unconscious, but just sort of mellow. If you can somehow get the monkey to place the barrel in his mouth that would be great too.

Now, remember: don't hesitate. Just pull the trigger.

You've thought a lot about this decision and, with a logical and sound mind decided it was what you wanted. Be aware going in that emotions can be difficult to handle and often make you question yourself in these situations. But press on.

You are going to shoot this monkey today.

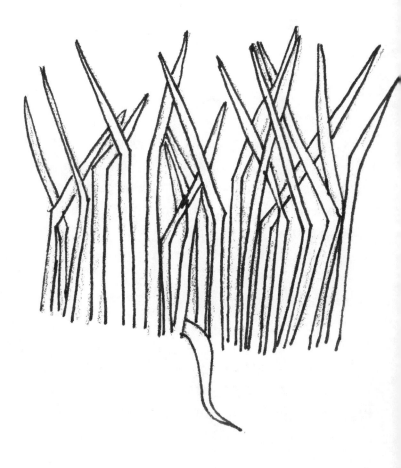

I SWEAR

No one would admit it, but I swear, seeing a garter snake in the grass while you walking along scared us kids half to death. Indeed, ourteen of us died that summer. Still, we would never admit it. People say I admitted it at a ball game one time, when what I really said was, "I bad hit it." I swear to you.

A FINE LINE

I wonder if serious sticker collectors count stamps into the grand total amount of stickers they have. Because that's walking a fine line don't you think?

CALM DOWN, ACCEPT THE TRUTH

If you get strapped into a straight jacked the first fear you'll have is that you'll get an itch in the crotch region you won't be able to reach. But that doesn't mean you're crazy. In fact, that's the sanest thought you've had all day.

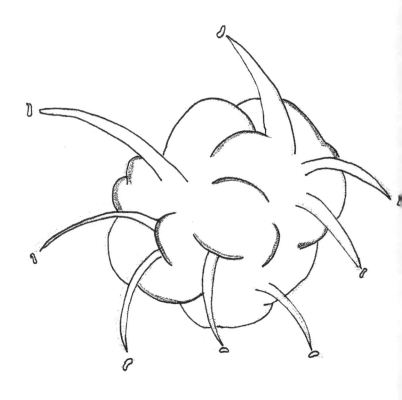

ADDED FLAIR

For suicide bombers; why not hold a week's worth of crap in as well, for added flair upon detonation.

ITS OWN REWARD

Back in olden times, probably the most rewarding chore of the day was getting to throw the slop water out into the street and hit passersby. They'd stand there drenched, looking up, smiling, pointing their finger at you. You'd be shrugging your shoulders, grinning, with a "guilty-as-charged" look on your face. It was their way of saying, "Hey, I kid around a lot, but it's just because I care."

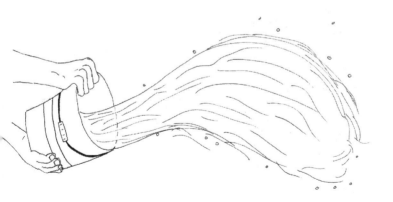

A MODEL

I like to go down to the mall and tape thimbles to mannequins to give them "outie" bellybuttons. That way, if someone with an outie sees one maybe they'll think, "You know what? Maybe I am normal."

"No, no," I'll say. "Those are thimbles."

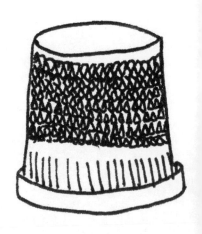

MAYBE IT WAS A CRAZY GOOD DEAL

Once they come out with a waterproof toaster, I bet they'll really look at you like you're nuts if you still buy the regular one.

THE PROPHECY OF NETHERTOTH

As young William wandered off the playground to fetch a ball, he came upon an ancient tree that seemed strangely out of place. Examining it closer, he discovered it was no ordinary tree at all, but a talking one. As William drew near, the tree magically came to life and spoke to him about times of old. Times of Kings and Queens, and Dark Lords with powers of sorcery that have not been matched in thousands of years. Then, the tree's face grew stern, for he spoke of the Great Prophecy of Nethertoth, and how the evil prince of the underworld would return one day to finally seek revenge on the blood descendant of King William of Loch.

"Uh, oh," William jumped up, "this tree's a dork." Returning to his dodge ball game quickly as to avoid 'dork association,' he never spoke of it again. However, years later, as a popular adult he would often ponder the events of that day and say, "Whew, that was close."

PRESSING ONWARD

Hard work, determination, never giving up. These are the words I use to describe myself when lying about gambling debt.

BUCKET LIST

If I were being sacrificed to a volcano by a bunch of
islanders, I hope it wouldn't be too offensive if I asked
them to 'hold up a sec,' so I could take a quick poop
directly into the orifice. Because I'm not ashamed to
say that's something I've always wanted to do.

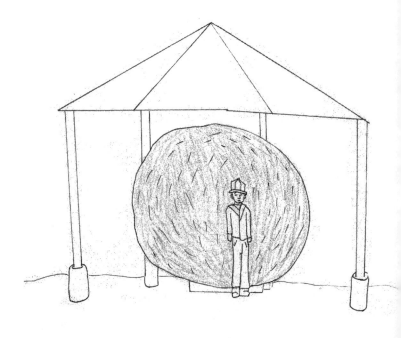

ON GREATNESS

You call the Cawker City, Kansas Twine Ball the, "Greatest Twine Ball Ever." But you don't have a clue do you? Have you not even considered my plans for a ball no less than 2 feet greater than Cawker? Seriously, I think you need to take a step back and reevaluate some things, -like about *life*. <u>That ball is *minuscule.*</u>

WAVE RIDER

I f I had a surfboard, I would name it "Wave Rider". Then, I would take it out and fail miserably in front of my peers. That night, I would burn "Wave Rider" in an abandoned garbage can to stay warm. But with the dawn would come a new day. A day when I would rise up, stand gazing out at the ocean, and say, "You really sucked out there yesterday, Wave Rider."

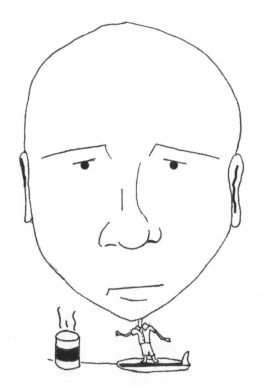

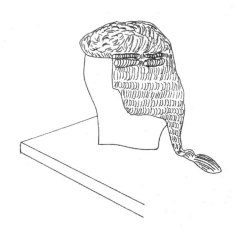

THAT'S POLITICS, BABY

If you are a powdered wig distributor in the fading days of the Whig party, you have got to ask yourself, what are you going to do with an entire warehouse full of these powdered wigs?! I mean, can you sell them back to the French or what?! Because they're starting to look so incredibly unnerving just sitting there in the warehouse!! Why did you get in this miserable business in the first place?!

THE WINDS CHIMETH

I like to stand at my neighbor's back door and gently blow on their wind chimes.   They lie in bed thinking, "The wind does not blow, and yet the chimes let forth their sound. What whimsical magic is afoot?" Tis I, thy neighbor. Go back to sleep.

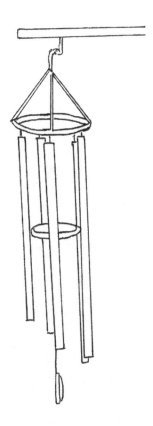

PERSPECTIVE

Then there were the times when they didn't think they'd make it. Later, they'd look back on those times to realize they were right. They didn't make it.

PARTY LIKE THERE'S NO TOMORROW

I always love a good, spirited rouse where people throw their wine glasses into the fire and cheer! Until the next day when everyone stands around in awkward silence as they watch the cleaning lady pick up the glass. "We're really sorry," everyone says, trying not to make eye contact.

JUST, STOP

I don't think we should bury our poet dreamers
underneath weeping willow trees,
because that's a bit much.

THE RUSH OF MEMORIES

Imagine you were raised by wolves and then rescued and assimilated back into society. Then, many years later in a far away town, you are by chance entered into a 'hands-free' turkey-eating contest. Ahh, can't you feel the rush of memories flooding back even now?

THANK YOU

To Jenni, Joe, and Lennon.

Also, to Jack Handey, the master of this craft.
And Nate Sadler, Jordan Green, Matt Donley, Jason
Steffens, Chad Gibbs, Charlie Rush, Mike Schwab,
Robert Casumbal, Jim Hope, Tom Johnson, Josh
Weinstein, Leigh Rubin, Matt Diffee, Scott Johnson,
Steve Berry, David Hall, Jill Bardwell, PJ Silva,
all my friends at No Shame Eugene,
and my dog, Rags.

Here's another bit I wrote about Rags:

Each day my dog would excitedly
bring me his leash to walk him.

It got easier to ignore
after about the fifth day.

Just kidding Rags, love ya buddy

DIDN'T HATE "WHAT WE ONCE CALLED OUT IN PASSING CLOUDS"?

Order the companion book *Good Chemistry* on Amazon.

"Dark and Hilarious, like dark chocolate. I guess I should have said chocolate that comes in really funny shapes."

-Jack Handey
Creator, Deep Thoughts

VISIT AARONDONLEY.COM

STILL WANT MORE?

Sign up for the Aaron Donley newsletter at aarondonley.com and receive Aaron's plans to increase Gideon Bible readership through strategically placed doodles:

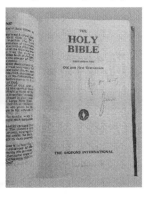

Dear Gideon Bible Folks, we've all been there: You're pacing around a sleazy motel room at 3 a.m. searching desperately for any type of porn, when you see a strategically placed, intricately styled doodle on the cover of the Gideon Bible...

WHY ARE YOU STILL HERE? ALL THE OTHER READERS HAVE GONE HOME TO THEIR HOT SIGNIFICANT OTHERS AND ADORING FAMILIES.

Ok, well if you'd like to leave a quick, honest review of this book it would be very much appreciated by both the author and Rags. :)

Made in the USA
Middletown, DE
20 August 2024